100 of the best quotes of Ron Swanson

Ron Swanson – Director of Parks and Recreation, Pawnee, Indiana

In this book you will find 100 of his best, most insightful quotes.

Enjoy reading them!

Chris Bennett

1

"The less I know about other people's affairs, the happier I am. I'm not interested in caring about people. I once worked with a guy for three years and never learned his name. Best friend I ever had. We still never talk sometimes."

2

"Dear frozen yogurt, you are the celery of desserts. Be ice cream or be nothing. Zero stars."

3

"When people get too chummy with me, I like to call them by the wrong name to let them know I don't really care about them."

4

"Give a man a fish and feed him for a day. Don't teach a man to fish... and feed yourself. He's a grown man. And fishing's not that hard."

5

"There's only one thing I hate more than lying: skim milk. Which is water that is lying about being milk."

"Give 100%. 110% is impossible. Only idiots recommend that."

7

"One rage every three months is permitted. Try not to hurt anyone who doesn't deserve it."

8

"Live your life how you want, but don't confuse drama with happiness."

9

"There has never been a sadness that can't be cured by breakfast food."

"Metaphors? I hate metaphors. That's why my favorite book is Moby Dick. No frufu symbolism, just a good simple tale about a man who hates an animal."

Ben Wyatt: "You know, you are a wonderful guy, and I admire many things about you, but you are a terrible person to discuss personal problems with."

Ron: "Thank you friend, that really means a lot to me."

12

"Fishing relaxes me. It's like yoga, except I still get to kill something."

"Do you have any history of mental illness in your family?" "I have an uncle who does yoga."

14

"Is Star Wars the one with the wizard boy?"

15

"Just give me all the bacon and eggs you have. Wait… I worry what you heard was, 'Give me a lot of bacon and eggs.' What I said was, give me all the bacon and eggs you have. Do you understand?"

"I love being a father but there are a few things I miss: Silence. The absence of noise. One single moment undisturbed by the sounds of a children's program called Doc McStuffins. There is no quiet anymore. There is only Doc McStuffins."

Ron: "And I'll have the number eight."

Server: "That's a party platter, it serves twelve people."

Ron: "I know what I'm about son."

Leslie: "Why would anybody ever eat anything besides breakfast food?"

Ron: "People are idiots, Leslie."

"I like Tom. He doesn't do a lot of work around here. He shows zero imitative. He's not a team player. He's never wanted to go that extra mile. Tom is exactly what I'm looking for in a government employee."

20

"If any of you need anything at all, too bad. Deal with your problems yourselves, like adults."

21

"What religion am I? Well I am practicing none of your damn business."

Ann Perkins: "You're stranded on a desert island, what is the one thing that you bring with you?"

Ron Swanson: "Silence."

23

"Leslie, my first wife Tammy, tried throwing me a surprise birthday party. When I saw my friends hiding through the window, I drove to a gas station, called the cops, and told 'em people had broken into my home. I'm not big on surprises."

24

"The government is a greedy piglet that suckles on a taxpayer's teat until they have sore, chapped nipples."

25

"I'd wish you the best of luck but I believe luck is a concept created by the weak to explain their failures."

"Capitalism is the only way... It makes America great, England OK and France terrible."

27

"Crying: Acceptable at funerals and the Grand Canyon."

28

"You had me at 'Meat Tornado.'"

"The Human Resources department requires that I be available once a month to discuss workplace disputes with my employees. The rules do not specify whether or not I am allowed to listen to Willie Nelson on my headphones."

"Barbecues should be about one thing: good shared meat."

31

[Ron does not subscribe to the new world of social media, and being on the grid.] "Food is for eating, places are for being. End of discussion."

"Fishing is for sport only. Fish meat is practically a vegetable."

33

"Put some alcohol in your mouth to block the words from coming out."

34

"I have a hernia. I've had it for a while, and I've been ignoring it successfully. But uh, this morning, I made the mistake of sneezing. But as long as I sit still and don't move my head or torso, I'm good. I got this."

35

"I'm impressed with Andy, pulling himself up by his bootstraps. Reminds me of a young me. I got my first job when I was nine working at a sheet metal factory. In two weeks I was running the floor. Child Labor Laws are ruining this country."

36

"I have never lied about anything in my life. Though, I suppose you could construe camouflage as a lie."

37

"I am not a sore loser. It's just that I prefer to win and when I don't, I get furious."

38

"On my deathbed, my final wish is to have my ex-wives rush to my side so I can use my dying breath to tell them both to go to hell one last time."

39

"The whole point of this country is if you want to eat garbage, balloon up to 600 pounds and die of a heart attack at 43, you can! You are free to do so. To me, that's beautiful."

40

"This is not government work, as such I treat it with care and attention."

41

"I also think it's pointless for a human to paint scenes of nature when they can just go outside and stand in it."

42

"I love Food and Stuff. It's where I buy all my food… and most of my stuff."

43

[Ron gives a gift to Chris] "The crib I built, I'm giving to you and Ann. It's perfectly safe. I tested it by hitting it with my truck."

44

"It's always a good idea to demonstrate to your coworkers that you are capable of withstanding a tremendous amount of pain."

[After being asked if he wants a salad]
"Since I am not a rabbit, no I do not."

46

"I can't think of anything more noble to go to war over, than bacon and eggs."

47

"Under my tutelage, you will grow from boys to men. From men into gladiators. And from gladiators into Swansons."

"Friends: one to three is sufficient."

49

"When I eat, it is the food that is scared."

"Strippers do nothing for me... but I will take a free breakfast buffet anytime, anyplace."

51

"There are only three ways to motivate people: money, fear, and hunger."

52

"Normally, if given the choice between doing something and nothing, I'd choose to do nothing. But I will do something if it helps someone else do nothing. I'd work all night, if it meant nothing got done."

53

"Breakfast food can serve many purposes."

"Sting like a bee. Do not float like a butterfly. That's ridiculous."

"I've cried twice in my life. Once when I was 7 and hit by a school bus. And then again when I heard that Li'l Sebastian had passed."

"Busy? Impossible. I work for the government."

"In my opinion, not enough people have looked their dinner in the eyes and considered the circle of life."

58

"I regret nothing. The end."

"I hope the rest of your day is cool beans."

60

"Don't start chasing applause and acclaim. That way lies madness."

61

"I call this turf 'n' turf. It's a 16-ounce T-bone and 24-ounce porterhouse. Also, whiskey and a cigar. I am going to consume all of this at the same time because I am a free American."

[Describing his allergies] "Cowardice and weak-willed men... and hazelnuts."

"Well I've never been one for meeting new people, or doing new things, or eating new types of food, or traveling outside of southern Indiana. I've had the same haircut since 1978 and I've driven the same car since 1991. I've used the same wooden comb for three decades. I have one bowl. I still get my milk delivered by horse."

"I assumed this was obvious but in the future, I'd prefer not to be part of any conversation about which body oil is best."

65

"Are you going to tell a man that he can't fart in his own car?"

"I don't want to paint with a broad brush here, but every single contractor in the world is a miserable, incompetent thief."

"Creativity is for people with glasses who like to lie."

"I've said it before and I'll say it again, children are terrible artists. And artists are crooks."

"Leslie, I got married twice, both times I was a lot older than those two, and both marriages ended in divorce and a burning effigy. Whose to say what works? You find somebody you like and you roll the dice. That's all anybody can do."

"I like some changes. Like when I change a tree into a canoe, or a wife into an ex-wife."

71

"Another word for 'jokes' is 'lies'. I do not lie. Therefore, I do not joke."

72

"There is only one bad word: taxes."

73

"If it doesn't have meat, it's a snack."

"Say what you want about organized religion, but those bastards knew how to construct an edifice."

[Describes his bowling technique]
"Straight down the middle. No hook. No spin. No fuss. Anything more and this becomes figure skating."

"Any dog under fifty pounds is a cat and cats are useless."

"That is a canvas sheet, the most versatile object known to man. It can be used to make tents, backpacks, shoes, stretchers, sails, tarpaulins, and I suppose, in the most dire of circumstances, it can be a surface on which to make art."

"I think that all government is a waster of taxpayer money. My dream is to have the park system privatized and run entirely by for-profit corporations, like Chuck E. Cheese. They have an impeccable business model."

"I would rather bleed out than sit here and talk about my feelings for 10 mins."

"Every two weeks I need to sand down my toe nails. They're too strong for clippers."

81

"Birthdays were invented by Hallmark to sell cards."

"Listen, I've eaten a commissary hamburger for lunch every day for twelve years. I just wanted to make sure this pointless health crusade won't affect the only part of my job that I like."

"I prefer quality over flash – that's why I refuse to write my signature in cursive."

"...if you believe in something you sign your name to it."

"The less I know about other people's affairs, the happier I am."

"I'm not interested in caring about people."

"There are three acceptable haircuts: high and tight, crew cut, buzz cut."

"The key to burning an ex-wife effigy is to dip it in paraffin wax and then toss the flaming bottle of isopropyl alcohol from a safe distance. Do not stand too close when you light an ex-wife effigy."

"I've created this office as a symbol of how I feel about government. This sawed-off shotgun belonged to a local bootlegger. People who come in here to ask me for things have to stare right down the barrel…"

"Veganism is the sad result of a morally corrupt mind. Reconsider your life."

"We will get along just fine, though hopefully not too fine because I am not looking for any new friends. End speech."

"There's a new wind blowing in government, and I don't like it. All of a sudden there's all this federal money coming in, and Paul the City Manager is telling us to build parks. Start new community programs. It's horrifying."

"Gentlemen, wilderness weekend is upon us. There will be no video games, there will be no internet pads. This weekend you have two parents, me and mother nature."

"My first ex-wife's name is Tammy. My second ex-wife's name is Tammy. My Mom's name is Tamara... she goes by Tammy."

"I work hard to make sure my department is as small and as ineffective as possible."

"History began on July 4, 1776.
Everything that happened before that
was a mistake."

"I'll take that steak to go. Please and thank you."

"Turkey can never beat cow."

"America: The only country that matters. If you want to experience other 'cultures,' use an atlas or a ham radio."

"An ideal night out, to me, is stepping onto my porch area and grilling up a thick slab of something's flesh and then popping in a highlight real from the WNBA."

101

"The only thing that's important at the end of the day is what's on your gravestone — your name."

"On nights like this when the cold winds blow, the air is awash in the swirling eddies of our dream, come with me and find safe haven in a warm bathtub full of my jazz."

"Great Job, Everyone. The Reception Will Be Held In Each Of Our Individual Houses, Alone."

"Never Half-A*s Two Things. Whole-A*s One Thing."

Printed in Great Britain
by Amazon